Reduce, Reuse, Recycle

Metal

Alexandra Fix

www.heinemann.co.uk/library
Visit our website to find out more information about **Heinemann Library** books.

To order:

☎ Phone ++44 (0)1865 888066

🖹 Send a fax to ++44 (0)1865 314091

💻 Visit the Heinemann Bookshop at www.heinemann.co.uk/library to browse our catalogue and order online.

First published in Great Britain by Heinemann Library, Halley Court, Jordan Hill, Oxford OX2 8EJ, part of Harcourt Education.
Heinemann is a registered trademark of Harcourt Education Ltd.

Editorial: Cassie Mayer and Diyan Leake
Design: Steven Mead and Debbie Oatley
Picture research: Ruth Blair
Production: Duncan Gilbert

Origination: Chroma Graphics (Overseas) Pte Ltd
Printed and bound in China by South China Printing Company Ltd

ISBN 978 0 431 90756 7
12 11 10 09 08
10 9 8 7 6 5 4 3 2 1

British Library Cataloguing in Publication Data
Fix, Alexandra, 1950-
Metal. - (Reduce, reuse, recycle)
1. Scrap metals - Juvenile literature 2. Scrap metals - Recycling - Juvenile literature 3. Waste minimization - Juvenile literature
I. Title
363.7'288

Acknowledgements
The publishers would like to thank the following for permission to reproduce photographs: Alamy pp. **7** (Leslie Garland Picture Library), **10** (Tom Payne), **15** (Imagebroker), 20 (Megapress), **21** (Nic Hamilton); Ardea pp. **9** (David Hancock), **25** (Jean Michel Labat); Corbis pp. **5** (Matt Rainey/Star Ledger), **8** (James L. Amos), **11** (Yang Liu), **12** (Latour Stephanie), **13** (Cheryl Diaz Meyer/Dallas Morning News), **14** (André Fichte/ Zefa), **23** (James L. Amos), **26** (Peter Beck), **27** (O. Alamany & E. Vicens), **28** (Lane Kennedy); Getty Images p. **19** (Photodisc Red); NHPA p. **4** (ANT Photo Library); Photolibrary.com pp. **6**, **16** (Plain Picture), **17** (Banana Stock), **18** (Phototake Inc.); Science Photo Library pp. **22** (Alex Bartel), **24** (Rosenfeld Images Ltd).

Cover photograph reproduced with permission of Corbis (Douglas Whyte).

The publishers would like to thank Simon Miller for his assistance in the preparation of this book.

Every effort has been made to contact copyright holders of any material reproduced in this book. Any omissions will be rectified in subsequent printings if notice is given to the publishers.

Contents

Some words are shown in bold, **like this**. You can find out what they mean by looking in the glossary.

What is metal waste?

Every day people use things made out of metal. People travel in cars and buses made of metal, drink juice from metal cans, and use metal forks and knives. Metal is an important material, but sometimes it is wasted.

To make metal, rocks must be dug from deep inside the earth.

4

Metal drink cans can be recycled.

Metal waste is metal that is thrown away.
If metal is reused or **recycled**, it can be
used over and over again. This would
waste less metal.

What is made of metal?

Many different items are made of metal. We use metal to make small items such as paper clips and drink cans. We use it to make large things such as cars, bridges, and buildings.

Most aeroplanes are made of metal.

Metal cans store fruit, vegetables, and soups.

Homes are filled with metal items such as canned foods. We often cover food with foil, and cook with metal pans.

Where does metal come from?

Metal comes from rocks **mined** from the ground. Metal is removed from the rocks by heating and melting them.

Rocks that provide metal are dug from the ground.

Bauxite is used to make aluminium.

The two most common metals are aluminium and steel. Aluminium comes from a rock called bauxite. Steel is made from iron ore rock and carbon. Carbon comes from coal.

Will we always have metal?

↑ This ship is carrying iron ore.

Aluminium is a **non-renewable resource**. Once this material is used up it will be gone forever.

Steel is made from two non-renewable resources: iron ore and coal. Coal is in shorter supply than iron ore and aluminum.

Steel is made by heating iron ore with coal.

What happens when we waste metal?

Metal waste is harmful to the **environment**. Some metal waste is buried in **landfills**. It may take hundreds of years for the metal to break down.

↑ Animals can get injured by waste metal.

Old aluminium cans break down into tiny metal pieces. These pieces can kill fish.

Steel is a type of metal that slowly breaks down and creates a powdery dust called **rust**. Rust can get into soil. It can then wash into nearby rivers and lakes and cut off sunlight to plants. This causes plants, fish, and tiny water animals to die.

How can we reduce metal waste?

The best way to reduce metal waste is to use less metal. Instead of buying drinks in metal cans, take a reusable drink container with you.

Mix drinks in a jug at home.

Buying fresh fruit and vegetables reduces metal waste from canned foods.

Buy fresh food whenever possible. Canned foods waste metal. If you do use food packaged in cans, buy larger cans. One large can wastes less metal than two small cans.

How can we reuse metal?

You can reduce metal waste by reusing metal. Share things made of metal with someone else. Give away bikes and toys that you no longer use.

Try to fix broken things instead of throwing them away.

Wash foil pans and use them again. ↑

You can also reuse small metal items for art projects. Make new containers by decorating used metal cans with paper or paint. These can hold your pencils, pens, crayons, or small toys.

How can we recycle metal?

Spray cans should be emptied but not squashed.

When metal is **recycled**, it is melted down and used again to make a new item. Most **communities** have a recycling programme for metal, paper, plastic, and glass.

After you have saved metal items, get them ready for recycling. First remove plastic lids and rinse out cans. Ask an adult to flatten aluminium cans.

Foil pieces should be rolled into a ball so the scraps are not lost.

Where can we take metal for recycling?

Some areas have **recycling** programmes. People can leave items in recycling bins for collection. A lorry comes to pick up the items to be recycled from each home.

Recycling lorries take materials to recycling centres.

Recycling centres have areas where you can sort different materials for recycling.

If your **community** does not have a recycling programme, you can take used drink cans to a supermarket. From there they are taken to a recycling centre. Household metal must be taken directly to a recycling centre.

How is metal recycled?

At a **recycling** centre, aluminium is separated from steel. Then the metals are packed into large bundles called bales. At the metal **factory**, bales are chopped into tiny pieces.

Large magnets pick up metal from other waste.

The pieces are melted in a very hot **furnace** to turn the metal into liquid. After the liquid metal is removed from the furnace it cools and hardens. The hardened metal is rolled out flat to use for new products.

Melted aluminium is poured and hardened into bars called ingots.

How do we use recycled metal?

Recycled metal can be used over and over again. Heavy steel can be reused to make car bodies, roofs, and small **appliances** such as toasters.

These sheets of steel will be used to make new items.

Flattened sheets of recycled steel can be used to make food cans.

Old aluminium drink cans are often recycled into the same thing. Foil wrappers can become wrappers again.

How can you take action?

You can help reduce metal waste. Ask family and friends to start **recycling** metal. You can help by rinsing out cans for recycling.

A good school project could be setting up a recycling container outside the school cafeteria.

Ask your teacher if your class and school can start recycling drink and food cans in the cafeteria. Find out where your local recycling centre is located. By reducing our own metal waste, we can help keep our planet clean.

Make a tin can telephone

Ask an adult to help you with this project.

1. Wash out two metal cans.
2. Ask an adult to punch a hole into the bottom of each can.

3. Cut a piece of string about 4.6 metres (5 yards) long.
4. Thread the string through each can and tie a knot at the ends.
5. Find a friend. Walk as far apart as you can so you stretch the string tight.
6. Hold the can to one person's ear, while the other person talks into the can. Take turns talking and listening.

Tin can telephones work in a similar way to real telephones. The vibrations of your voice travel from one can down the tight string into the other can.

Glossary

appliance	household machine, such as a dishwasher or toaster, that usually runs on electricity or gas
community	group of people who live in one area
environment	natural surroundings for people, animals, and plants
factory	building or buildings where something is made
furnace	closed-off space that is heated at high temperatures to warm a building or melt solid materials
landfill site	large area where rubbish is dumped, crushed, and covered with soil
mine	dig out a material that lies deep in the earth
non-renewable resource	material taken from the earth that cannot be replaced by nature
recycle	break down a material and use it again to make a new product. Recycling is the act of breaking down a material and using it again.
rust	reddish-brown coating that forms when iron or steel starts to break down

Find out more

Books to read

How We Use Materials: Metal, Rita Storey and Holly Wallace (Franklin Watts, 2006)

Using Materials: How We Use Metal, Chris Oxlade (Raintree, 2005)

Why Should I Recycle? Jen Green (Hodder Wayland, 2002).

Websites

Waste Watch work to teach people about reducing, reusing, and recycling waste. You can visit www.recyclezone.org.uk to find out more information about waste and to try some online activities..

Find out where you can recycle in your local area at: www.recyclenow.com by typing in your postcode. You can also find out more about which items can be recycled, more facts about waste, and what you can do to help!

Index